CALL OF THE HEART

40 Days Devotional

Call of the heart to encourage and inspire
throughout one's faith journey,
wherever they may be on their journey
for everyday focus living.

Life begins when the mind receives the word of God;
and allow it to govern its thoughts and behavior.

Let this mind be in you, which was also in Christ Jesus.
—Philippians 2:5 KJV

Shirley Steele

ISBN 979-8-88832-466-0 (paperback)
ISBN 979-8-88832-467-7 (digital)

Christian Faith Publishing
832 Park Avenue
Meadville, PA 16335
www.christianfaithpublishing.com

Printed in the United States of America

DAY 1

In the beginning God created the heaven
and the earth. And the earth was without form,
and void; and darkness was upon the face of the
deep. And the Spirit of God moved upon the face
of the waters. And God said, Let there be light:
and there was light. (Genesis 1:1–3 KJV)

If God's words created the heavens and earth, what do you think His
words can do for you?

Just because you don't see it does not mean that He has not or
will not do it. Your level of belief is the key to how much you will
experience what He has provided for you, let alone the additional
things He provided for you just because you asked. So don't let your
blind spot distract you from your destiny! Keep on trusting, and He
will deliver as promised.

DAY 2

> The Lord by wisdom hath founded the earth;
> by understanding hath he established the heavens.
> (Proverbs 3:19 KJV)

When it comes to changing our current situation, most of us lack the skill and not the courage. Do not succumb to the serenity prayer, "God, allow me to give up because I don't understand or cannot distinguish the times," just because you do not have the skills to overcome the present circumstance or situation. Seek the wisdom to change it, then the circumstance or situation will surrender or yield to your applied wisdom (faith).

> My people perish, are destroyed by the lack
> of knowledge. (Hosea 4:6 KJV)

Don't get trapped in surrendering because this is different than what you've faced before when wisdom was what you needed. Seek what makes it different, then apply that knowledge to make it an opportunity for success. Anything that is different and/or even difficult can open up a world of opportunity.

Be an opportunist! This may not be the season for courage but the season for knowledge.

> God gave Solomon great wisdom and under-
> standing, and knowledge to prosper, he was the
> riches King in all the earth. (1 Kings 4:29 and 1
> Kings 10:23 KJV)

This book of the law shall not depart from your mouth, but you shall meditate on it day and night, so that you may be careful to do according to all that is written in it; for then you will make your way prosperous, and then you will have success. (Joshua 1:8 NASB)

You were born a winner, and winners never quit!

DAY 3

Enter into his gates with thanksgiving, and
into his courts with praise: be thankful unto him,
and bless his name. (Psalm 100:4 KJV)

Praises will get you through heaven's doors. If you have not been receiving, it may be because you have not been praising.

Don't seek God; come into His presence
with the problem, seek God with the solution;
the Garment of Praise. For God knows what you
are in need of before you ask.

Therefore do not worry, saying, "What will
we eat?" or "What will we drink?" or "What will
we wear?" For it is the Gentiles who strive for
all these things; and indeed your heavenly Father
knows that you need all these things. But strive
first for the kingdom of God[a] and his[b] righteousness, and all these things will be given to
you as well. (Matthew 6:31–33 NRSV)

Eye hath not seen, nor ear heard, neither
have entered into the heart of man, the things
which God hath prepared for them that love
him. (1 Corinthians 2:9 NKJV)

God blows your mind with his marvelous blessings, so much that you or no one else could have imagined. If you are not a person of praise, you will never experience it.

DAY 4

As it is written in the prophet Isaiah, "See! I am sending my messenger ahead of you, who will prepare your way." (Mark 1:2 ISV)

Do not get discouraged, lose heart, or be envious of those that come before you. There were some that came before Jesus and His ministry. Those that come before you help cultivate the harvest so that you may reap where you have not sown. Take what you need and leave the rest either in letter or deed for others to help them on their journey.

"I sent you to reap that for which you did not labor. Others have labored, and you have entered into their labor." (John 4:38 ESV)

Then she left, and went and gleaned in the field after the reapers. And she happened to come to the part of the field belonging to Boaz, who was of the family of Elimelech. (Ruth 2:3 NKJV)

DAY 5

And whoever shall not receive you, nor hear your words, when you depart out of that house or city, shake off the dust of your feet. (Matthew 10:14 ASV)

In passing, we may encounter some people who form opinions about us—opinions that do not measure up to our true authenticity. Through passing, they may have caught word of your speech or action and taken it out of context and not the fullness of your being. They hold on to your flaws or mistakes and dismiss the unseen substance of your beauty. For God Himself said that you are the apple of His eye (Zechariah 2:8 KJV), fearfully and wonderfully made (Psalm 139:14 KJV).

We all have had times when we were misjudged or represented. You are not at fault of how others perceive you; they are! One's thoughts belong to one. Just as beauty (or not) and wisdom to discern beyond the surface is in the eye of the beholder. If they can't see you, then you are not meant to be seen by them—keep passing.

DAY 6

> Trust in the LORD with all thine heart; and lean not unto thine own understanding. In all thy ways acknowledge him, and he shall direct thy paths. (Proverbs 3:5–6 KJV)

Trusting in the Lord is a time of testing. This past weekend, I decided to get my car washed. I pulled up to the car wash, and as I proceeded to drive in, a man stood before the entranceway with a sign that said, "Place car in neutral."

Neutral…wow. Have you ever researched the meaning of that word? Yeah, I know you know what neutral means, but have you really looked at this word—*neutral*? **It means not helping or supporting either side in a conflict, disagreement, etc.; impartial. Not taking part or giving assistance.**

So I did. With caution, I held on to the steering wheel. The man seemed to have had a frenzy because my hands were still on the wheel. His eyes lit up as he firmly looked at me, and then he pointed to the next sign a little way up that read, "Hands off wheel." I slowly released my hands from the steering wheel and allowed my car to move along the guided rails but wanted to take hold again once I got inside of the car wash. I couldn't see where I was going for the soap suds. That big cloth hitting against my car and the noise from the washing can be a little frightening. Neither could I accelerate nor reverse my car because I didn't know what was behind or in front of me, and I didn't want to run into something or damage my car. So I submitted to obeying the instructions, and before I knew it, I was through safely to the other side.

To acknowledge God is to give Him permission (admit to belonging to Him) to handle the situation.

A lot of the time, when circumstances that appear to be unfavorable show up in our lives, we say to God, "I need You," or "Where are You?" And God replies in a calm, still voice, "I am here. Place yourself in neutral, get your hands off the wheel, do not accelerate [get ahead] or go in reverse [go back or behind]. I will see you through."

DAY 7

If any man will come after me (desire or to know me intimately), let him deny himself (apply discipline behavior; faith) and take up his cross (pursue his purpose) daily and follow me (enter into my rest where my yoke is easy and my burdens is light. (Luke 9:23 KJV and Matthew 11:30 KJV)

Chase after the truth like all hell and you'll free yourself, even though you never touch its coattails. (Clarence Darrow)

But you will be transformed!

Do not be conformed to this world, but be transformed by the renewal of your mind, that by testing you may discern what is the will of God, what is good and acceptable and perfect. (Romans 12:2 ESV)

DAY 8

The sacrifices of God are a broken spirit; a
broken and contrite heart, O God, you will not
despise. (Psalm 51:17 KJV)

There's a cost to humility: you have to be willing to let go of yourself, your personal desires, and even self-pity. Pick up your cross and walk, for must Jesus bear the cross alone and the whole world go free?

Most statements that begin with "I am" is self-serving. There's only one I Am, and that is the Lord. So we don't own the rights to these words. There are no copyrights, and you won't get any of the royalties. We are not the legal owner of the words "I am," so don't expect anything from it because you won't get paid. Serve the Lord with all your heart, all your mind, and all your soul.

A broken spirit and a contrite heart are humble servants, who release I Am to who is the "I Am that I Am" (Exodus 3:14 KJV).

What broke David were the words that came out of prophet Nathan's mouth: "For the word of God is living and active, sharper than a two-edged sword piercing to the dividing of soul and spirit, of joints and marrow, and discerning the thoughts and intentions of the heart."

If the Word doesn't do anything to you, you are already dead—the walking dead.

We are broken for we have sinned, but I am not ashamed of the Gospel, for it is the Gospel that sets us free (2 Samuel 11:14–15 KJV and 2 Samuel 12:7 KJV).

DAY 9

Then he said to me, "Fear not, Daniel, for
from the first day that you set your heart to understand and humbled yourself before your God,
your words have been heard, and I have come
because of your words. The prince of the kingdom of Persia withstood me twenty-one days, but
Michael, one of the chief princes, came to help
me, for I was left there with the kings of Persia."
(Daniel 10:12–13 ESV)

Beloved, when the thing you desire rests in your heart and is no longer disturbed by outside influences (self or others), that is when you
will receive it.

When we fear, it summons the enemy. Fear is the war cry for
the enemy and holds up our blessings, while hope and praise is the
war cry for our Father God. You can rest your heart in the surety of
God's sovereignty, supreme power, and/or authority. When we put
our hope in other things, we lose our peace and delay our blessings.

For God hath not given us the spirit of fear;
but of power, and of love, and of a sound mind.
(2 Timothy 1:7 KJV)

DAY 10

And no one puts new wine into old wineskins. For the wine would burst the wineskins,
and the wine and the skins would both be lost.
New wine calls for new wineskins. (Mark 2:22
NLT)

Don't force it to fit.

You know that you have outgrown your current position when
the small things frustrate you. Things that you may have enjoyed in
the past. It's like trying to fit your foot in that beautiful old size 8
shoe that you wore for years. But now, without you even being aware
of it, your foot grew, and you now wear a size 8 ½ or 9. Don't force
it to fit. If you do, you may cause harm to the foot (yourself) and/
or the shoe (other people around you). Follow the anointing (Holy
Spirit)!

You can find just as many beautiful shoes in a size 9 as you did
in a size 8.

DAY 11

Become that which you strive to obtain.

> Before you can have, you must do; but before you can do, you must first become. (Tommy Newberry, *Success Is Not an Accident*)

You can't have an outer body experience until you first have an inner body experience. Inner and outer body experiences are not only spiritual, they are physical as well. Faith is the outward reflection or experience of an inward belief.

> But the fruit (outer body) of the Spirit (inner body) is love, joy, peace, patience, kindness, goodness, faithfulness, 23 gentleness, self-control; against such things there is no law. (Galatians 5:22–23 ESV)

To produce the fruit, you must first have the seed. You must become peace (the seed) to experience peace (the fruit), just as you must become healthy to experience good health. You can't sow curses and expect to reap blessings. And neither can you sow what you don't have. If you want to get a different fruit, you must change your seed. To change your seed, learn what you desire to have, then become what you have learned and sow it.

In other words, you can't possess what you don't have unless you obtain what you desire to possess.

DAY 12

I really enjoy listening to Tasha Cobbs Leonard's song "Fill Me Up Lord," don't you? However, sometimes when we are praying and asking God to fill us up, we fail to actually experience fulfillment.

Well, that maybe because we have too much in us! He can't fill us up until we get rid of what we have (cast our cares).

> Humble yourselves (let go of what you have) therefore under the mighty hand of God, that he may exalt you (fill you up) in due time: Casting all your care upon him; for he careth for you. (1 Peter 5:6–7KJV)

Have you ever eaten and found that you still are not full or satisfied? That feeling when you are doing something that should lead to fulfillment, but for some reason or another, you can't seem to get fulfillment fast.

You have too much in you! You can't fill a cup with water when the cup is already full. That water has to be released somehow to either half or completely empty. It's only when the water has been emptied out or when the cup has been given room can you pour into it or fill it up again. The only problem with not fully emptying the cup before you attempt to add to it is that what is already in the cup will affect that which is trying to enter the cup, and that could be either good or bad depending on the substance there.

You have to release that which is filling you up: doubt, worries, loneliness, pride, greed, guilt, lies, confusion, illnesses, lust, depression, anxiety, strongholds of any kind, and most of all, self and/or anything that is keeping you from focusing on God. Fasting can empty you of these things that may have held you captive so that God can fill you up again with His desires and His will for your life.

It is only when we have emptied ourselves can we really experience true fulfillment.

Lord, help me to empty myself, then "Fill me up, Lord, fill me up."

DAY 13

> But when he saw the wind boisterous, he was
> afraid; and beginning to sink, he cried, saying,
> Lord, save me. And immediately Jesus stretched
> forth his hand, and caught him, and said unto
> him, O thou of little faith, wherefore didst thou
> doubt? And when they were come into the ship,
> the wind ceased. (Matthew 14:30–32 KJV)

You don't have to pray for God to give you peace. You already have peace. Just keep the peace that you have. At times you may feel an uncontrolled emotion or misdirected energy as though you don't have peace. This may be because you let go of the peace that you possessed. Don't let go of your peace! Peace can and should become your attitude, demeanor, and/or character so that when you come into an area of life that may be a bit confusing, destructive, or tempestuous, your demeanor will demand the tempest wave to calm or cease. Jesus said to Peter, "Wherefore didst thou doubt." In other words, why have you let go of or surrendered your peace? Peace summons reverence of honor when it is not forsaken.

> Peace I leave with you, my peace I give unto
> you: not as the world giveth, give I unto you.
> Let not your heart be troubled, (uncontrolled
> emotion or misdirected energy) neither let it be
> afraid. (John 14:27 KJV)

DAY 14

> Now in the fourth watch of the night Jesus went to them, walking on the sea. And when the disciples saw Him walking on the sea, they were troubled, saying, "It is a ghost!" And they cried out for fear. But immediately Jesus spoke to them, saying, "Be of good cheer! It is I; do not be afraid." And Peter answered Him and said, "Lord, if it is You, command me to come to You on the water." So He said, "Come." And when Peter had come down out of the boat, he walked on the water to go to Jesus. (Matthew 14:25–29 NKJV)

Peter had the audacity to ask the maker of all things to prove himself. The "I am that I am" to prove that he is! First, I thought, *Who does Peter think he is, asking the Lord to prove himself?* But then I realized that Peter did this because he knew that Jesus wouldn't disappoint him.

What do you do when life circumstances and/or situations ask you to prove yourself; when you show up, and that which you showed up to asks you to prove yourself? That job or position that you want, that relationship, money, home, or car (prosperity). Do you just say, "Forget it. If they don't know by now, then they won't know"? Or do you show them what you are working with? When you know who you are and whose you are, you won't mind proving it.

So the next time life challenges you to show it who's in authority, don't shy back or withdraw from the challenge. Rise to the challenge as Jesus did. Show it just what it's asking for and command it to walk give to you what you desire.

DAY 15

Casting all your care upon him; for he careth for you. (1 Peter 5:7 KJV)

The Lord will perfect that which concerneth me: thy mercy, O Lord, endureth forever: forsake not the works of thine own hands. (Psalm 138:8 KJV)

What does this mean to you? "Cast your cares upon the Lord, for He will perfect that which concerns you." I know it seems simple in words, but sometimes the simplicity of a thing is missed and life is lost.

Cast: to throw away from or to push or shove off.
Cares: all things, good or bad, that are in your heart that distract or resist the Word of God to cause anxiety, impatience, worry, and/or distress, resulting in an impaired vision or success.
Perfect: to produce or perform to the fullest with no loss or without the things that have defect or could cause you injury or hindrance to success.

Praise casts out cares as a form of sowing. You sow your cares in exchange for God's good (His perfecting/His perfect will).

Push off the world's yoke, take off like dirty soil laundry so that you can receive your coat from the Father which is a perfect fit and will not weight you down but be liberating, and take the yoke of God, for He is the burden bearer. Our shoulders are not broad enough to carrier it, so we have to be okay with that because some jobs require only one man.

> Come unto me, all ye that labour and are heavy laden, and I will give you rest. Take my yoke upon you, and learn of me; for I am meek and lowly in heart: and ye shall find rest unto your souls. For my yoke is easy, and my burden is light. (Matthew 11:28–30 KJV)

> I will bless you with a future filled with hope—a future of success, not of suffering. (Jeremiah 29:11 CEV)

DAY 16

Let this mind be in you, which was also in
Christ Jesus. (Philippians 2:5 KJV)

Jesus spoke His father's thoughts. These thoughts were words that brought life and not death so that our joy could be filled.

> For I have not spoken of myself; but the Father which sent me, he gave me a command-ment, what I should say, and what I should speak. (John 12:49 KJV)

> These things have I spoken unto you, that my joy might remain in you, and that your joy might be full. (John 15:11 KJV)

If you are experiencing a lack of joy, check your thoughts. Your thoughts are like Hansel and Gretel dropping breadcrumbs on the trail to your destiny.

Kryptonite would destroy or render Superman helpless, and so will not having the right mind or having bad or wrong thoughts. The mind (the entirety of thoughts) is like the outer shell of a walnut that holds all thoughts. Sometimes it may release one thought or many thoughts, which can be the energy, force, or fuel to the resulted path or future. Sometimes the shell looks good, but the inside is rotten. The inside of the mind (thoughts) is exposed by the fruit it bears.

> A good tree cannot bring forth evil fruit,
> neither can a corrupt tree bring forth good fruit.

Every tree that bringeth not forth good fruit is hewn down, and cast into the fire. Wherefore by their fruits ye shall know them. (Matthew 7:18–20 KJV)

You have heard it said before, "You are what you think." For as he thinketh in his heart, so is he: Eat and drink, saith he to thee; but his heart is not with thee. (Proverbs 23:7 KJV)

Your mind holds the power to your end!

Keep thy heart (mind) with all diligence; for out of it are the issues of life (your resulted end). (Proverbs 4:23 KJV)

DAY 17

All Scripture is breathed out by God and profitable for teaching, for reproof, for correction, and for training in righteousness, that the man of God may be complete, equipped for every good work. (2 Timothy 3:16–17 ESV)

When we do not accept the whole word of God, we are operating in partiality or being double-minded.

Some may choose to only govern themselves by the Old Testament covenant promises such as not eating certain foods. And then there are some who choose to only govern themselves by the New Testament covenant promises such as eating all things, forgetting that if eating all things may cause another to stumble, sin, or fall, he should not do so, believing he is free to do what he wants.

A bondman or a slave can be free, but a freeman or a servant cannot be bound. The difference between a slave (Old Testament) and a servant (New Testament) is that one is forced or is given his position while the other humbly accepts or chooses his position.

As my son said, "God has developed your faith, now he is keeping your faith." So with that being said, the Old Testament may get you there, but the New Testament keeps you there, and in that, there is no partiality. Accept all of the word; in doing so, you will experience the fullness of God through having a relationship with Christ Jesus, his son.

Looking unto Jesus the author and finisher of our faith; who for the joy that was set before him endured the cross, despising the shame, and is set down at the right hand of the throne of God. (Hebrews 12:2 KJV)

DAY 18

You have not because you ask not; asking is another way of proclaiming truths (your inheritance). When you know that something belongs to you, you ask in a different mindset. You ask with a knowledge that "because this is mine, I can't be turned down." Most items that have been bought have a receipt of purchase. Jesus's shed blood is your receipt of purchase, that what you ask for you will receive, not because of you but because of Him.

Hitherto have ye *asked nothing in my name: ask, and ye shall receive, that your joy may be full.* (John 16:24)

And this is the confidence that we have in him, that, *if we ask any thing according to his will, he heareth us.* (1 John 5:14 KJV)

And whatsoever ye shall ask in my name, that will I do, that the Father may be glorified in the Son. If ye shall ask any thing in my name, I will do it. (John 14:13–14 KJV)

Sons and Daughters of the Most High God, do not beg and plead. They ask and believe. Know who you are and whose you are. For in Christ Jesus you are all sons of God, through faith. (Galatians 3:26 KJV)

Don't forget to ask. It's your inheritance.

DAY 19

Be still, and know that I am God: I will be
exalted among the heathen, I will be exalted in
the earth. (Psalm 46:10 KJV)

Believe what you know instead of what I see.

Stop looking anxiously at the storm; problem waiting for it to pass instead turn your back
to the storm and look until the hills from where
your help comes from. (Psalm 121:1–3 ESV)

You give respect, which is a form of praise, to what has your
attention. Looking at the storm, waiting for it to pass, can cause that
storm to change from just a cloud to rain, hail, tornado, and maybe
even a hurricane. The weather person may tell the ones that are in the
radar of a storm to pack up and leave the premises.

Focusing on your issues gives it power, just
as the serpent was once a snake but then became
a dragon. (Revelation 12:9 KJV)

Anything that has our attention gets the
praise and praise is the fire that ignites the flames.
Learn to be anxious for nothing but in all things
give God the praise. (Philippians 4:6–7 ESV)

I will set no wicked thing *before mine eyes*: I
hate the work of them that turn aside; it shall not
cleave to me. (Psalm 101:3 KJV)

DAY 20

But God, being rich in mercy, because of the great love with which he loved us, even when we were dead in our trespasses, made us alive together with Christ—by grace you have been saved. (Ephesians 2:4–5 ESV)

Great is God's mercy toward us. His love and kindness he's shown us. It hasn't always been easy in relationships—marriage, job, children, health, money, family, and friends—but you are still here because of God's mercy, despite of all the challenges and setbacks!

You have a mercy testimony! We all do; and with it, we are loose from our bonds. Our testimonies untie the soul and free us to live another day in faith of our coming Lord Jesus Christ. It's the oil in our lamps and the flame in our eyes that give us hope in times of trouble.

And they overcame him by the blood of
the Lamb, and by the word of their testimony;
and they loved not their lives unto the death.
(Revelation 12:11 KJV)

But the wise took oil in their vessels with
their lamps. (Matthew 25:4 KJV)

There's a song called "How I Got Over" by Mahalia Jackson. The verse says, "You know my soul look back and wonder how I made it over." We go through and get over by our testimonies. Tell your testimonies. You never know who's listening or waiting to hear your testimony so that they can break free!

DAY 21

But *without faith* (the son) it is impossible to please him (the father): for he that cometh to God must believe that he is, and that he is a rewarder of them that diligently seek him. (Hebrews 11:6 KJV)

Faith is neither a so-called feeling we get, nor is it small enough for the world's *Merriam-Webster Dictionary* to define. Faith, when used biblically as **a spirit**, can only be defined by the Holy Spirit, who teaches us all truth. Meaning, faith is beyond reasoning.

That your faith should not stand in the wisdom of men, but in the power of God. But the natural man receiveth not the things of the Spirit of God: for they are foolishness unto him: neither can he know them, because they are spiritually discerned. (1 Corinthians 2:5 and 14 KJV)

Jesus saith unto him, "I am the way, the truth, and the life: **no man cometh unto the Father, but by me**." (John 14:6 KJV)

You can't please the Father without the Son.

Faith comes by hearing and **hearing the word of the Lord**. (Romans 10:17 KJV)

What—or better yet, Who—is the Word of the Lord that we are to hear?

> And the **Word was made flesh**, and dwelt among us, (and we beheld his glory, the glory as of the only begotten of the Father), full of grace and truth. (John 1:14 KJV)

> And there was a cloud that overshadowed them: and a voice came out of the cloud, saying, This is **my beloved Son: hear him**. And suddenly, when they had looked round about, they saw no man anymore, save **Jesus only** with themselves. (Mark 9:7–8 KJV)

"Faith without works is dead" (James 2:16 KJV). What works are we to do? This does not always mean that you have to physically do something. It depends on what is required for the substance that is at hand—an offering and/or sacrifice as did Abraham—at the moment of faith testing. This work could be to stay constant or, as much as possible, in belief (working out your own salvation [Philippians 2:12 KJV]); and if your offering or sacrifice is the right one and you still do not see it—JUST TRUST. Trusting will sail you through to the other side, and you may just realize that you really didn't need it at all, or you had just enough for the journey.

Simply put, faith means believing that God will do what He says He will do. He who has God's heart **(the Word)** does not lack for his arm.

> Being confident of this very thing, that he which hath begun a good work in you will perform it until the day of Jesus Christ. (Philippians 1:6 KJV)

Something to think about: if He will perform it until the day of Jesus Christ, then to have mature faith, to me, is death from the body (to be absent from the body is to be present with the Lord). So if you feel as though your faith is smaller than a mustard seed, don't worry. You still have a lot of living to do.

"FAITH IS A JOURNEY, NOT A GUILT TRIP." This journey is your never-ending walk with God.

DAY 22

Are you your brother's and/or sister's keeper?

> Receive us; we have wronged no man, we
> have corrupted no man, we have defrauded no
> man. (2 Corinthians 7:2 KJV)

> Bear ye one another's burdens, and so fulfil
> the law of Christ. (Galatians 6:2 KJV)

What you did may have not been wrong, but how you handled what you did may have been wrong. Whether you're right or wrong, if you hurt another special fellow Christian, then your right was wrong.

There is no such a thing as self-promotion. "True humility is not to belittle oneself but instead it is to not think of oneself at all" (Joyce Meyers). When one reduces him or herself to love, it's the only thing that is present.

> I know and am persuaded in the Lord Jesus
> that nothing is unclean in itself, but it is unclean
> for anyone who thinks it unclean. For if your
> brother is grieved by what you eat, you are no
> longer walking in love, (Romans 14:14–15 ESV)

DAY 23

Never demand or expect more of others than you do of yourself. The measure (judgment/expectations) you give will be the measure (judgment/expectations) you will receive. If you are not able to receive it, then don't give it.

> Do to others whatever you would like them to do to you. This is the essence of all that is taught in the law and the prophets. (Matthew 7:12 NLT)

> For with what judgment ye judge, ye shall be judged: and with what measure ye mete, it shall be measured to you again. (Matthew 7:2 KJV)

If you want to be heard, be a better listener.
If you want to be a leader, be a better follower.
If you want a good friend, be a better friend.
If you want to be forgiven, forgive others.
If you want to be blessed, be a blessing.
If you want to be trusted, show yourself trustworthy.

> Be the salt in your own flavor. Ye are the salt of the earth: but if the salt have lost his savour, wherewith shall it be salted? (Matthew 5:13 KJV)

DAY 24

Beloved, if you cannot believe it, you cannot receive it!

> Therefore, I tell you, whatever you ask for
> in prayer, believe that you have received it, and it
> will be yours. (Mark 11:24 NIV)

Believe until victory or believe until death; either way, you will win if you do not stop believing. Believing gives us strength in areas where we lack or had none. But beware, it has a price tag. The cost is doubt. You must relinquish doubt so you can believe. Only one king can sit on the throne, so decide which king, doubt or belief, you will allow to govern your life. One brings confusion, and the other gives you peace.

DAY 25

Little children, you are from God and have
overcome them, for he who is in you is greater
than he who is in the world. (1 John 4:4 ESV)

There will always be something to overcome (produce virtue)—people, places, and things. However, the key to overcoming or producing virtue is to overcome or be virtuous. A person who remains optimistic will always succeed. It is when we close this channel that we forfeit our right to produce virtue and fail to manifest our true image.

DAY 26

Anything that God has given you, you will not lose. The body (vessel) that once held what was dear to your heart may no longer be with you this season; however, the spirit of it is not lost. The spirit of love, joy, peace, patience, kindness, goodness, faithfulness, gentleness, and self-control is still here.

People may forget what you said, but oftentimes they do not forget what you did or how you made them feel. So you see, life (love) never dies. The flesh (sin) of that life does, but love lives forever.

> But the Holy Spirit produces this kind of fruit in our lives: love, joy, peace, patience, kindness, goodness, faithfulness, gentleness, and self-control. There is no law against these things! (Galatians 5:22–23 NLT)

> If I had the gift of prophecy, and if I understood all of God's secret plans and possessed all knowledge, and if I had such faith that I could move mountains, but didn't love others, I would be nothing. (1 Corinthians 13:2 NLT)

Note: The scripture (Galatians 5:22–23 KJV) spiritually reads as so: "The Holy Spirit produces Love and the spirit of love is joy, peace, patience, kindness, goodness, faithfulness, gentleness, and self-control. Sin [death] cannot and will prevail against the Spirit of Love [life]!"

You who have the Spirit of the Lord dwelling within you, the gates of hell will not prevail against or overtake you!

> And I say also unto thee, That thou art
> Peter, and upon this rock I will build my church;
> and the gates of hell shall not prevail against it.
> (Matthew 16:18 KJV)

You have nothing if you do not have love!

DAY 27

Have you heard the saying "Evil do what evil does?" It means that if someone is evil, they will do evil things. They will carry through on their threats or intentions.

Continuous consumption of such in any manner can alter one's belief and behavior. Guard the pathway to your soul with the things of God; what goes in is what will come out.

> Finally, brethren, whatever is true, whatever is honorable, whatever is right, whatever is pure, whatever is lovely, whatever is of good repute, if there is any excellence and if anything worthy of praise, dwell on these things. The things you have learned and received and heard and seen in me, practice these things, and the God of peace will be with you. (Philippians 4:8–9 NASB)

DAY 28

As the famous words of gospel singers Mary Mary, "Go get your blessing."

> Notwithstanding, lest we should offend them,
> *go thou to the sea, and cast an hook, and take up the*
> *fish that first cometh up; and when thou hast opened*
> *his mouth, thou shalt find a piece of money: that take,*
> *and give unto them for me and thee.* (Matthew 17:27
> KJV)

God has told you where the blessing is, so now go and get it! Sure, you may have to go into some unfamiliar places, the water may be bone chilling cold, and it may be scary, but don't fret for God is with you!

> Now the LORD had said unto Abram, Get
> thee out of thy country, and from thy kindred,
> and from thy father's house, unto a land that I
> will shew thee. (Genesis 12:1 KJV)

Ask yourselves, "How hungry am I for the blessing?" Are you hungry enough to go and get it?

> For thou shalt eat the labor of thine hands:
> happy shalt thou be, and it shall be well with
> thee. (Psalm 128:2 KJV)

Just think about it—it's yours for the taking, and as soon as you take it, the drought will be over!

DAY 29

Never trust yourself to yourself, relying on your own abilities. Always trust yourself to God!

You did not make yourself, so you can not define yourself. If we do, we will fall short of or limit ourselves.

> Then God said, Let us make mankind in our image, in our likeness. (Genesis 1:26 KJV)

> Before I formed you in the womb I knew you, and before you were born I consecrated you; I appointed you a prophet to the nations. (Jeremiah 1:5 NASB)

> But Jesus beheld them, and said unto them, With men this is impossible; but with God all things are possible. (Matthew 19:26 KJV)

The possible can only exist when we surrender the impossible.

DAY 30

Therefore you shall be perfect, just as your
Father in heaven is perfect. (Matthew 5:48 NKJV)

But above all these things put on love, which
is the bond of perfection, (Colossians 3:14)

To be perfect is not of one's actions. Perfect is of one's being. It's the state of a sound mind, free from worldly attributes—a clear conscience. There is no fear, injury in love because perfect love casts out fear, injury. For fear has to do with punishment. Whoever fears (resides in injury) has not been perfected and has his conscience cleared in love.

There is no fear in love. But perfect love
drives out fear, because fear has to do with punishment. The one who fears is not made perfect
in love. (1 John 4:18 NASB)

For God has not given us a spirit of fear,
but of power and of love and of a sound mind (2
Timothy 1:7 KJV)

DAY 31

> For consider your calling, brothers: not many of you were wise according to worldly standards, not many were powerful, not many were of noble birth. But God chose what is foolish in the world to shame the wise; God chose what is weak in the world to shame the strong; God chose what is low and despised in the world, even things that are not, to bring to nothing things that are. (1 Corinthians 1:26–28 ESV)

Your purpose and calling in life have two different aspects. Your purpose is whatever is at hand in that hour—a plan or goal. However, your calling in life is that which you are weakest in but have a desire to do. If God blessed you in your purpose (an on-the-job promotion), you will never get to your calling. Your purpose is there to help you, but your calling is there to help others.

We are not doing nothing if we are not doing what we were called to do!

"God does not call the equipped. Instead, He equips those He calls."

> For we are his workmanship, created in Christ Jesus for good works, which God prepared beforehand, that we should walk in them. (Ephesians 2:10 ESV)

To equip the saints for the work of ministry, for building up the body of Christ. (Ephesians 4:12 ESV)

To this end we always pray for you, that our God may make you worthy of his calling and may fulfill every resolve for good and every work of faith by his power. (2 Thessalonians 1:11 ESV)

DAY 32

Your word is a lamp to my feet and a light
to my path. (Psalm 119:105 ESV)

Hold on to the revelation word, for it is the light unto your path. The hidden truths to an open, free soul. With revelation, you will master, manage, or steward life's dictations during the moment of trial as the processor of virtue and wisdom.

DAY 33

The works of faith is always present in the life of one who is aware of His presence. Who is faith?

Faith is God, and God is faith, so trust your faith! Faith will never lead you astray, a wilderness without provision. However, you will surely go astray if you don't have Jesus, for faith without works, Jesus is dead!

> Looking unto Jesus the author (the beginning) and finisher (the end) of our faith. (Hebrews 12:2 KJV)

> For as the body without spirit is dead, so faith without works is dead also. (James 2:26 KJV)

DAY 34

This is the day that the Lord has made; let
us rejoice and be glad in it. (Psalm 118:24 ESV)

Stop waiting on life the way you would prefer things to be. Stop waiting to start living but, rather, live the life that you have.

To enjoy my life, I thought this meant waiting until things changed or got better. But instead, to enjoy life—I am learning—means just that! Enjoy life as it is no matter what. The good, the bad, and the ugly.

In Philippians 4:11–12 KJV, Paul said, "Not that I speak in respect of want: for I have learned, in whatsoever state I am, therewith to be content. I know both how to be abased, and I know how to abound: everywhere and in all things. I am instructed both to be full and to be hungry, both to abound and to suffer need."

If all you have is a little flour, only a couple of eggs, small thing of sugar, salt, and butter or oil (either one will do), you can make something enjoyable.

You can enjoy what the enemy meant for bad. In other words, "if life gives you lemons, make lemonade"—one of my sons' favorite quotes.

So while you are waiting on life, life is being lived, so you might as well enjoy it.

DAY 35

> Forgive for if you forgive others their trespasses, your heavenly Father will also forgive you, but if you do not forgive others their trespasses, neither will your Father forgive your trespasses. (Matthew 6:14–15 ESV)

To forgive is to excuse the act of the wrong brought against you—to release from an obligation, to permit to leave or overlook an offense or fault, to excuse or pardon sin.

Forgiveness in the Old Testament all carried with them the sense of removal of sin and the restoration of the relationship which was damaged by sin. In all cases, this forgiveness is conditional upon repentances, a changing of the mind and will, the act of not placing judgment against or upon someone.

In the New Testament, *a proper relationship with God* is also contingent upon forgiveness of sins. *Jesus instructed His disciples to practice forgiveness without limitation—until seventy times.* Seventy *(always forgiving)* means completion or perfection, so forgive until it's forgiven, for without this willingness to forgive, there could be no forgiveness of their own sins.

When you forgive someone, self, or incident, will you still hurt? Will you still remember what you have forgiven?

When it's forgiven, you will still remember it, but with a different view or expression of action. Now instead of remembering it with the action or emotion of hurt or disappointment, it will be more of a gratitude or peace, the emotion or action changed. You can be at peace with the trespass another apposed upon you.

Stress or depression is a form of unforgiveness. Stress or depression is held in or trapped offences or emotions that the stressed or depressed person has not excused or released (renewed mind). This has caused them to be imprisoned (bondage) in another person or one's actions.

Every time those old or unpleasant thoughts come up, cast them down as many times as it takes to release the power of forgiveness. Change your view.

> Casting down imaginations, and every high thing that exalteth itself against the knowledge of God, and bringing into captivity every thought to the obedience of Christ. (2 Corinthians 10:5 KJV)

Forgiving is the practice of refocusing or adjusting the thoughts that cause the hurt, stress, disappointment, depression, or offense that will change your action.

DAY 36

A Saint is just a sinner who failed down but got up.
—Donnie McClurkin

No matter who's at fault, learning how to get up after the fall (mistakes and/or failure of any kind) is part of the process.

> For the righteous falls seven times and rises again, but the wicked stumble in times of calamity. (Proverbs 24:16 ESV)

Seven is the number of completeness and perfection, both physical and spiritual. Meaning, you can be subject or put to the test several times in a particular area until you develop the desired fruit that the seed produces. So don't get offended or fret when you fail; it's for the furthering of the Gospel. Someone is watching you and how you get up because they are looking to you for guidance in their faith journey.

> Filled with the fruit of righteousness that comes through Jesus Christ, to the glory and praise of God. I want you to know, brothers, that what has happened to me has really served to advance the gospel. (Philippians 1:11–12 ESV)

DAY 37

A man's mind plans his way [as he journeys through life], but the Lord directs his steps and establishes them. (Proverbs 16:9 AMP)

Plans dictate life and place order or demand the end to a day or future. A lot of our lives are out of order or have no directions because we failed to plan. If we have an attitude of "whatever comes," then whatever will come. That is why we experience so many failed desires or disastrous days, feeling as though nothing was accomplished.

How can you accomplish anything if you do not set something before you to accomplish. If you do not have a destination, then you could end up anywhere.

God cannot give you guidance or direction if you have not presented Him with a plan. Don't come to the party empty-handed.

DAY 38

But this command I gave them: "Obey my voice, and I will be your God, and you shall be my people. And walk in all the way that I command you, that it may be well with you." (Jeremiah 7:23 ESV)

And Samuel said, "Has the LORD as great delight in burnt offerings and sacrifices, as in obeying the voice of the LORD? Behold, to obey is better than sacrifice, and to listen than the fat of rams." (1 Samuel 15:22 ESV)

Sometimes the only obedience is to believe what God has spoken about a particular situation or circumstance. If He said that it is temporary, your obedience to His response is to believe as so, it is temporary. If you don't, then you will experience the season longer than what He had planned for you. You prolonged your deliverance, not God. Obey the Word and live in the fruit that the obedience produced.

DAY 39

"Then the kingdom of heaven shall be likened to ten virgins who took their lamps and went out to meet the bridegroom. Now five of them were wise, and five *were* foolish. Those who *were* foolish took their lamps and took no oil with them, but the wise took oil in their vessels with their lamps. But while the bridegroom was delayed, they all slumbered and slept. And at midnight a cry was *heard:* 'Behold, the bridegroom is coming; go out to meet him!' Then all those virgins arose and trimmed their lamps. And the foolish said to the wise, 'Give us *some* of your oil, for our lamps are going out.' But the wise answered, saying, '*No,* lest there should not be enough for us and you; but go rather to those who sell, and buy for yourselves.' And while they went to buy, the bridegroom came, and those who were ready went in with him to the wedding; and the door was shut. Afterward the other virgins came also, saying, 'Lord, Lord, open to us!' But he answered and said, 'Assuredly, I say to you, I do not know you.'" (Matthew 25:1–12 NKJV)

How you treat yourself is how you treat God. If you put yourself last, you're putting God last. You're putting other people ahead of God—the God who is within you because you are God's representation. In your life, you got to put yourself first so that you can put God first.

During one of Oprah's life lessons sessions, a statement was said that what is in your cup is for you, and what overflows from that cup is for others. When you give that which causes you to sacrifice (give out of what you have in the cup without having an overflow, barely enough for yourself), you make those that you give to a thief. They are taking from what is available only to you and not to them. A thief takes what does not belong to them. If your cup is not overflowing, you can't give because there's no overflow to give. It's only enough for your journey.

DAY 40

You are the light of the world. A city set on
a hill cannot be hidden. Nor do people light a
lamp and put it under a basket, but on a stand,
and it gives light to all in the house. In the same
way, let your light shine before others, so that
they may see your good works and give glory to
your Father who is in heaven. (Matthew 5:14–16
ESV)

You are light; it is the image of God displayed when one is genuine
or true to oneself. Everyone carries their light differently. Some may
carry it in their eyes, and others may carry it in their smile. Light is
not just a skin complexion or visibility. It is an attitude or personality
that comforts or make others better. God created you this way, so
allow your uniqueness to guide you and others through to what is
destined.

ABOUT THE AUTHOR

Shirley Steele is a motivational speaker and a minister of the Word of God who received her undergraduate degree in pastoral ministry and Christian education from New Orleans Baptist Theological Seminary. Shirley is known as an effective communicator who works with individuals and organizations to amplify their impact on how they hear the Word of God concerning their walk with life through God's Word.

Shirley has served many years in the corporate industry by connecting with others and building their confidence so they can make an influential impact in this world. She mentors with passion, guiding people to effectively strengthen and elevate their lives and vision by gaining new insight.

Shirley desires to influence others through her ministry. Her friends and family will describe Shirley as humble, quick to listen, and a true woman of God who loves the Lord. She is admired and loved by many.

Shirley is a native of Atlanta, Georgia, and is proud parent to two adult sons, Michael and Shaquille, and grandchildren.